LITTLE MOUSE'S LEARN-AND-PLAY

Opposites

For a free color catalog describing Gareth Stevens' list of high-quality books and multimedia programs, call 1-800-542-2595 (USA) or 1-800-461-9120 (Canada). Gareth Stevens Publishing's Fax: (414) 225-0377. See our catalog, too, on the World Wide Web: http://gsinc.com

Library of Congress Cataloging-in-Publication Data

Dena, Anaël.
    [Contraires. English]
    Opposites / text by Anaël Dena ; illustrated by Christel Desmoinaux.
       p. cm. — (Little Mouse's learn-and-play)
    Summary: Text, illustrations, and simple activities introduce the
concept of opposites.
    ISBN 0-8368-1987-X (lib. bdg)
    1. English language—Synonyms and antonyms—Juvenile literature.
    [1. English language—Synonyms and antonyms.] I. Desmoinaux, Christel, ill.
II. Title. III. Series: Dena, Anaël. Little Mouse's learn-and-play.
PE1591.D4413 1997
428.1—dc21   97-14784

This North American edition first published in 1997 by
Gareth Stevens Publishing
1555 North RiverCenter Drive, Suite 201
Milwaukee, Wisconsin 53212 USA

This U.S. edition © 1997 by Gareth Stevens, Inc. Original © 1996 by Editions Nathan,
Paris, France. Titre de l'edition originale (original title): *Les Contraires* publiée par
Les Editions Nathan, Paris. Additional end matter © 1997 by Gareth Stevens, Inc.

Translated from the French by Janet Neis.
U.S. editors: Patricia Lantier-Sampon and Rita Reitci
Editorial assistant: Diane Laska

Printed in the United States of America

1 2 3 4 5 6 7 8 9 01 00 99 98 97

LITTLE MOUSE'S LEARN-AND-PLAY

Opposites

by Anaël Dena
Illustrated by Christel Desmoinaux

Gareth Stevens Publishing
MILWAUKEE

Tall - short

Little Mike is **short**.

His father, Max, is **tall**.

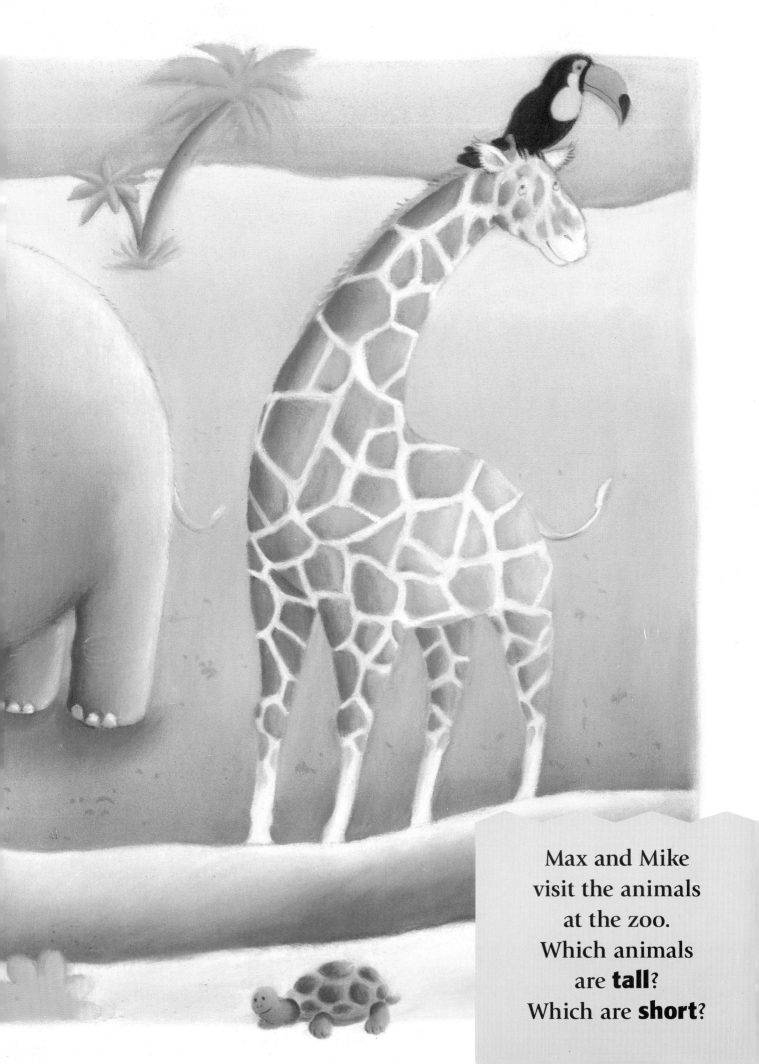

Max and Mike
visit the animals
at the zoo.
Which animals
are **tall**?
Which are **short**?

Full - empty

Charlene has eaten all her candy.

Her pockets are **empty**.

Charles' pockets are **full** of candy.

"Don't worry," he tells Charlene.

"We'll share."

Match the pictures showing the same objects **empty** and **full**.

Wide - narrow

Bobby's sweater is much too **wide**. Ben's sweater is much too **narrow**. Will his buttons pop?

The little cats must move this furniture into the house. Which things will fit through the **narrow** door? Which need to go through the **wide** window?

Long - short

Queen Kitty loves **long** dresses.
"Long dresses are pretty,"
she tells her husband.
King Cat always answers,
"Yes, but I prefer my
clothes **short**!"

Can you find any **short** things in the palace? What things are **long**?

Many - few

Joey has **many** coins in his piggy bank. Harry has **few** coins. He is generous and buys things for his friends.

Who has **many** things in the pictures above? Who has **few**?

Fat - thin

David is **fat**. His
brother Dan is **thin**.
They are both happy
to be that way.

Which bed is Dan's and which is David's? Who owns the other things in the room?

Slow - fast

Jeremy is **slow**. He is
usually late. Jenny is **fast**.
She is always on time.
This makes her teacher happy!

What things
go **slow**?
What things
go **fast**?

Open - close

Fran does her homework.
Her eyes are wide **open**.
Freddie's eyes are **closed**.
He is asleep on his notebook!

Can you find things
that are **open**?
What things
are **closed**?

Cold - hot

Amy went outside in her
nightgown. "Brrr, it's **cold**
out here!" she tells her friend.
"Oh, I'm so **hot**," says Alice, who
is wearing all her winter clothes!

Which things in
these pictures
do you think
are **hot**, and
which are **cold**?

Clean - dirty

Brian is **dirty**.
He doesn't care how
he eats. Brad doesn't
spill things on himself.
He is neat and **clean**.

Which things in
the dining room
are **clean**?
Which are **dirty**?
Which dog belongs
to Brian?

Soft - prickly

Look at all the presents! There is something for everyone. Carrie hugs her new **soft** doll. Curt prefers his **prickly** porcupine.

Which things in this
room are **soft**, and
which are **prickly**?

Happy - upset

Lou is **happy**. He took care of his flowers, and they grew well. Lisa is **upset**. Her bicycle has a flat tire. How will she get home?

Who is **happy**, and who is **upset**?

Wet - dry

Tina is **wet**. She put
on a raincoat to play in
the rain. Tony is **dry**.
He waits under the awning
for the rain to stop.

The rain **wet** nearly everything, but some places are **dry**. Can you find them?

Facing toward - facing away

Marna is **facing away** from class to draw on the chalkboard. The teacher is **facing toward** the class to read a book.

Who is **facing toward** the board?
Who is **facing away** from the board?

On - under

The cats are playing hide-and-seek. Tom hides **on** the cabinet. Todd looks for him **under** the couch!

Which things in the room are **on** something? Which are **under** something?

Inside - outside

What is making
that squeaky noise?
"Stay **inside**," says Marty.
But Michael wants to
see what is **outside**.

Which things in the pictures above are **inside** and which are **outside**?

High - low

Samantha likes to swing **high** in the sky. Sally prefers to stay **low**, near the ground.

Which characters and objects are **high**? Which are **low**?

In front - behind

"Please line up in order!"
says the photographer.
Paul goes to the **front** row,
but he is too tall. Pat is
behind Paul and won't
be seen in the picture.

For the class picture, the photographer said, "Short cats **in front**, tall cats **behind** them." Did all the cats obey? Which ones are in the wrong place?

Opposites, Opposites

Look at the two pictures to answer the questions below.

Who is **short** and who is **tall**?

Who is **thin** and who is **fat**?

Who is **behind**? Who is **in front**?

Who **faces toward**? Who **faces away**?

Who is **low**? Who is **high**?

Who is **clean**? Who is **dirty**?

What is **many**? What is **few**?

What is **wide**? What is **narrow**?

Did you find all the **opposites**?

The opposite game

Rules of the game:
To play, you need one game piece per person and one die. Place the game pieces on START. Each player takes a turn rolling the die and moving the number of spaces shown.

START

Cold

Short/Small

Slow

Outside

Upset

Narrow

Closed

Tall/Big

Empty

Low

Under

Facing awa

Look at the square you land on. Name its opposite. If you can't name the opposite, move back one space. The winner is the player who gets to FINISH first.

Books

Clifford's Word Book. Norman Bridwell (Scholastic)

Dinosaur Mad Libs. Leonard Stern & Roger Price (Price Stern Sloan)

First Word Books: Opposites. Neil Ricklen (Simon and Schuster Children's)

Fly with the Birds. Richard Edwards (Orchard Books Watts)

Language Brain Boosters. Becky Daniel (Good Apple)

My Big Book of Words. Isabel Clark (Smithmark)

My Book of Opposites. Beth A. Wise (McClanahan Book Co.)

My Silly Book of Opposites. Amerikaner (Silver Burdett Press)

My Wonderful Word Box. Tim Healy (Reader's Digest Association)

Pups Speak Up. Maxine Meltzer (Simon and Schuster Children's)

Science Buzzwords series. Karen Bryant-Mole (Gareth Stevens)

Six Thick Thumbs. Steve Charney (Troll Communications)

Videos

Clifford's Fun with Opposites. (Family Entertainment)

We Learn About Words. (Video Knowledge)

Words and Pictures. 7 programs. (Public Media, Inc.)

Words That Rhyme. (Coronet, The Multimedia/MTI Film and Video)

Yes-No — Stop-Go. (AIMS Media)

Web Sites

www.bonus.com/ (*See* Parents & Teachers, Fun for Young Kids, Play with Balloons)

www.bonus.com/ (*See* Parents & Teachers, Fun for Young Kids, Fishy Names)

Glossary – Index

awning: a rooflike cover over or in front of a window or building. Awnings can serve as shelters from rain or intense sun *(p. 30)*.

cabinet: a case or cupboard with doors and shelves *(p. 34)*.

chalkboard: a large, hard surface used in a classroom for writing or drawing on with chalk *(p. 32)*.

coin: a flat, round piece of metal used as money *(p. 14)*.

couch: a wide piece of furniture for sitting or lying down *(p. 34)*.

die: a small cube marked on each side with dots from one to six, usually used in pairs called dice *(p. 44)*.

furniture: movable objects, such as tables and chairs, used for living in a room or a house *(p. 11)*.

generous: unselfish and willing to share *(p. 14)*.

homework: schoolwork to be done at home *(p. 20)*.

match: to find two or more objects that look alike or have something in common, such as a color or a shape *(p. 9)*.

notebook: a book with blank pages in which to write *(p. 20)*.

object: anything that can be seen or touched *(p. 9)*.

opposite: two ends, or extremes, of qualities or things; things that are directly across from, or contrary to, one another. Example: hot and cold are the two extremes of temperature *(pp. 42, 44, 45)*.

palace: a very large, rich house for a king, queen, or other head of a country *(p. 13)*.

photographer: a person who takes pictures, or photographs, with a camera *(pp. 40, 41)*.

porcupine: a large rodent that has sharp, stiff spines for protection. The North American porcupine climbs trees, lives in woods, and is active at night *(p. 26)*.

raincoat: a coat that is waterproof *(p. 30)*.

share: to allow another to have or use something belonging to you *(p. 8)*.

zoo: a collection of living animals for display; short for zoological garden *(p. 7)*.